Whipped
Yara "Grace"

Acknowledgments

Dana: If you are reading this, then my chapbook got published. I know we will both be thrilled now eating, singing and dancing in my room. I want you to know that I will always love you.

Ms. Ola: You are my first teacher, my mentor and my rock. I hope you are proud of me. Whatever is thriving is because of you.

Maya: You are my mother, my aunt and my friend. I will always be your little girl. I will always love you.

Bakr: You are my dad. Your tenderness can heal the whole world. Thank you for being my real father.

Grandma: To me, you never died. I only recognize it when I write about you using the "past" sometimes. I loved you. I love you. Forgive me. I miss you.

Sarah: You were the **first** person I ever opened up to. Thank you for being there for me. It changed me in many ways. I love you.

Dr. Mohamed Youssef: No one has ever tolerated me like you. Thank you for your patience and understanding. You make me a better person. Thank you for never giving up on me.

Sameh: One day, I will read your book too. You pushed me to become who I am today. Thank you for being so kind to me. I hope the poems touch your beautiful heart.

Nick Baguley: Thank you for always being there for me. I couldn't have made it without you.

Stephen Reilly: I trusted you with my writings. I opened up to you...sometimes with worry, but you never let me down.

Omar: Without philosophy and without misery, we're nothing. Without you and without your kindness, I may not have made it.

Alaa: I'll always have your back knowing you'd always have mine. We've got our little secret too.

Salma: I couldn't have imagined a better book cover!

HIM: You gave me life …you breathed life into me. You touched a whipped. You're my first love. You're mine.

My Students: You gave me life. I love each one of you.

To all the *whipped*...

To Grace
& Gracie, too

Contents

SILENCE 1

HEAR 2

SHE/HE 3

LOVE 4

Dye 5

Grieving 6

To Him 7

Making Love 8

Feelings 9

Blood 10

Built 11

Redhead 12

Disappointment 13

Remember 14

Fetus 15

Blood (2) 16

The Tribe 17

Kiss Me 18

Swallow 19

Defendant 20

(_____) 21

Feed 22

(1) 23

(2) 24

Rope 25

Break Up.. 26

Background Music 27

First Step: Lay Down 28

INSOMNIA 29

Why 30

SILENCE

Talk to me about silence
Without breaking the walls
Whisper to me the words
That will break my heart
Unlock the rhythm in my soul
Play the notes
Feel the breakage
I don't know what you meant
I only feel
I could see
The discordance
Of your notes
The breaking of my heart
The splitting of my soul
All upon
Your touch
Set me free.

HEAR

I still hear the ringing of the bell
The ticking of the door's knob
The clicking of the lighter
The sound of his lips
I still see
Pens and papers on his desk
The window and the curtain
My nail polish and his chemise
The carpet and the table
I still smell
His cigarettes in me

All over the room
His perfume pulling me
Into his chest
I still feel
Very insecure
Yet embraced
Afraid
Yet craving more
I still feel
His hands on me
I still hear
The shovels against the wall.

SHE/HE

She was talking from a place he once visited
Unknowingly
He was responding spontaneously
Without pondering
The emotions at the tip of her lashes
She wanted a start over
He wanted a continuation
Both refused to mention
Where they tripped
He was a forgiver
She was a visitor of scars
Turning them into wounds
Burning the bones
Reaching the core
She was
Sophisticated
And he was
A figment of her imagination...

LOVE

I fell out of love
The way an infant gets weaned
I fell out of fullness
To real utter emptiness
The space gets occupied
A healthy occupation
The true self emerges
And gets rubbed off
Knots fall bleeding
The heart feels a hype
Numbness
Then goes wild
The soul ruptures willingly
And stays inside
The air is contaminated
The veins are pulled and scarred
The points are missed, unsolved
I fell in love
With a jar.

Dye

She dyes her hair
To hide her face
She looks down
To swallow the shame
She avoids handshakes
To prevent flashbacks
Her vision is distorted
Her existence is doubted
The only thing she draws
Is a dead fetus
She never talks.

Grieving

He's grieving over his mother
Through fabrics
Young beautiful women
Changing colors like the moon sometimes
He's grieving by being fussy
Anxiously meticulous
Deceitful if committed
He's grieving through wellness
Prosperity and all else
When sick, he's almost true
He's almost…partly himself
Almost loveable
Almost human
(There..she falls for him)

To Him

I visit him
Beg him to stop the bleeding
The wound he so cautiously constructed
I tell him the story
Of his coming,
The veins he touched,
Those he slit
I beg him to look at me
To hurt me more
To do anything
He hugs me silently
I bleed excessively.

Making Love

We thought we'd fill each other's holes by making love
He used to ask me to say certain words to him
All during making love
Sometimes after too
Honestly all the time, he needed to
I needed to
For the first time,
I lost my shyness
I asked him to tell me some words too
We made love for many days
For many months
At first, we were cured
But then, each hole kept leaking
I drowned
He floated
We separated for the first time
We got sick
Then attempted suicide
Across my table, he sits
Asking me to make love to him
Again.

Feelings

Some feelings are not true
Some feelings are not feelings
Mere flashbacks
Dragging you into the past
Denials of a brutal time
Iron handcuffs
Burnt lamps
Visions of near humans
Bracelets with vows
Fire kindled near the tent
There is my lover
Fire within my heart
Untrue feeling
No timeline.

Blood

The organized disarray
The sensitive numbness
Flinching softness
Of their skin
Their names, unreal
Same pattern
Different destruct
The blood in the air
Is not the end
This undeciphered trauma
Will go on
Till air spits blood
Till a DNA is checked
Till eternity
And beyond
Sensitive numbness
Rivers of blood.

Built

I built it
With his aid
My feelings are the walls
His defraud the ceiling
A shelter filled with fear
My bosom, his lust
My words…in the air
Approach, escape
Approach, give in
The walls are not in place
All skin smells of sin
Need and hollowness
The walls break in
His hand over my waist
My hands reaching his wrist
I give in…again and again
The fortress fades in.

Redhead

The redhead enchanted
The hopeless romantic
The color of blood
Darker than dream
The vision of the house
Is so unclear
His face from a distance
Stern and still
The redhead unconscious
Denial within.

Disappointment

The disappointment in her eyes
The weakness in her voice
The concealed incessant begging
For a glimpse of his attention
Her screaming hands
Only get touched
When unwanted
His arrogance
Shallowness
Senselessness
Is irksome
Persistent
Relentless
Free from pride
She lingers
Unrecognized,
She walks around the room
Careless,
He eats his asparagus.

Remember

I remember him
Standing at the edge
Asking for a lovely mistake
I remember her
Ripping all the edges
Jumping from a bridge
That is definitely man-made
I remember them all
But I let go of many
I remember everything
Just like today.

Fetus

It's a dead fetus
With slim arms
Tight closed eyes
She wraps it with a white towel
Kneels looking at the ground
Hands it to the mother
And says
"You got what you want".

Blood (2)

There is blood within the curtain
And the needles in that gown
The one you deem a dress
There is blood in the white knitted gown
I still wear
You can't see
All I hold
Are things unfree.

The Tribe

Tell the tribe of the deceased
The widowed and the divorced
That we are taking no more cries
That we are no more accepting grief
Tell the tribe of the female
Of the figure of the deceased
That we're not in mourn
And not in love
We're not escaping
The truth right here
Tell the tribe
Of the figure of the deceased
There is no funeral
There is no deceased.

Kiss Me

Kiss me till I bleed
Hug me till my bosom feels your beat
Let me be safe
Melt at your gaze
Kiss me so hard
I'm a woman between your arms.

Swallow

I swallowed all you gave me
No water needed
I ate all the lies
Rotten, tasteless
I met who you are
With my ashes
You buried me
Cold blooded
Oblivious that I
Declared my death
Beforehand.

Defendant

Where is the defendant
And the witness of love
Where are the words
Of lure and trust
Where are the convicted
Of loving and feeling
How do they look
Into each other's eyes
How do they forgive
Every moment in their past
How do they go on
Thinking
That this is the case
And we are the judges
Take a glimpse
Of the jury's eyes
Everybody knows
This is a lie
Except for them.

(____)

He touched me, I detached.

Feed

I wanted you to feed me something
Because I've never been fed
Couldn't you have given me some more?
Couldn't you have been generous?
Even when lying
A miser
Even with lies.
(They trap you)

(1)

Bring me wrath
Miscarriage and disappointment
Wrap me and scream
My heart in my spleen
Needles all over
Ripped, found to be numb
He runs in my veins
His air colonized me.

(2)

Grapes and glasses
Scarves and garments
Shouts and cries
Cages and locks
All verdicts thoroughly heard
Just fall with axe and a doll
Don't talk as there will be none
Humor me with silence
Or lose your breath on scream
I haven't witnessed anything
Nothing you feel is seen.

Rope

A rope convoluted
Around my heart
Smothering me for feeling
Blaming me for living
A perfume in my blouse
Reminding me of a feeling
Holding to my hands
I breathe it
And feel them both
Fear and love
I take the end of the rope
And tighten it
I feel the knot
I watch the bleeding.

Break Up

Like break ups
Unfinished haircuts
Unpoured tears
Unsaid words
Like an unfinished kiss
An undrunk beer
The incomplete drawing
Of an eyeliner
Like an unfinished meal
Unfinished love
An incomplete letter
Justifying the heart break
Like an unfinished cigarette
An open-ended movie
I am bleeding for you
Would you please…complete?
Would you please…kill me?

Background Music

Background music
Broken strings
It goes on
The playing goes on
I float between
The unplayed tones
I don't forget
I merely touch
The unused string
It breaks my heart
The hidden tone
Shatters my heart
Breaks my strings
I rest as ashes
With no strings
The playing goes on
There's a hidden tone still.

First Step: Lay Down

I lay down
And give him my flesh
I refused before
Because it meant something
I was preserving something
Taking care of it
There was something
Refusing to be bought this way
But now there isn't
Nothing is to be taken care of
Nothing is worthy of my care
And my flesh
Is just like me
Nothing
So I gave him something
Something he really wanted
But... In fact, it was nothing.

INSOMNIA

Fumble through the long night hours
Feel the distress
It feels like home sometimes
It feels a mess
What's wrong with the crack?
Why do you keep fidgeting?
Isn't it embedded?
Folding a sheet you need
Uncoil slowly
Fetch the inside
You had words inside you
You broke up.

Why

He said I was vulnerable
This is why I felt
That I needed a man
The truth is
I was always vulnerable
Especially with a man.

Printed in Great Britain
by Amazon

47181568R00024